101 Things I Learned in Architecture School

THE MIT PRESS   CAMBRIDGE, MASSACHUSETTS   LONDON, ENGLAND

Matthew Frederick

101 Things I Learned in Architecture School

MIT Press books may be purchased at special quantity discounts for business or sales promotional use. For information, please e-mail <special_sales@mitpress.mit.edu>.

This book was set in Helvetica Neue by The MIT Press. Printed and bound in China.

Library of Congress Cataloging-in-Publication Data

Frederick, Matthew.
101 things I learned in architecture school / by Matthew Frederick.
   p. cm.
ISBN-13: 978-0-262-06266-4 (hc : alk. paper)
1. Architecture—Study and teaching. 2. Architectural design—Study and teaching. I. Title. II. Title: One hundred one things I learned in architecture school. III. Title: One hundred and one things I learned in architecture school.

NA2000.F74 2007
720—dc22

                                                                                      2006037130

20 19 18 17 16 15 14 13 12 11 10

To Sorche, for making this and much more possible

Author's Note

Certainties for architecture students are few. The architecture curriculum is a perplexing and unruly beast, involving long hours, dense texts, and frequently obtuse instruction. If the lessons of architecture are fascinating (and they are), they are also fraught with so many exceptions and caveats that students can easily wonder if there is anything concrete to learn about architecture at all.

The nebulousness of architectural instruction is largely necessary. Architecture is, after all, a creative field, and it is understandably difficult for instructors of design to concretize lesson plans out of fear of imposing unnecessary limits on the creative process. The resulting open-enedness provides students a ride down many fascinating new avenues, but often with a feeling that architecture is built on quicksand rather than on solid earth.

This book aims to firm up the foundation of the architecture studio by providing rallying points upon which the design process may thrive. The following lessons in design, drawing, creative process, and presentation first came to me as barely discernible glimmers through the fog of my own education. But in the years I have spent since as a practitioner and educator, they have become surely brighter and clearer. And the questions they address have remained the central questions of architectural education: my own students show me again and again that the questions and confusions of architecture school are near universal.

I invite you to leave this book open on the desktop as you work in the studio, to keep in your coat pocket to read on public transit, and to peruse randomly when in need of a jump-start in solving an architectural design problem. Whatever you do with the lessons that follow, be grateful that I am not around to point out the innumerable exceptions and caveats to each of them.

Matthew Frederick, Architect
August 2007

Acknowledgments

Many thanks to Deborah Cantor-Adams; Julian Chang; Roger Conover; Derek George; Yasuyo Iguchi; Terry Lamoureux; Jim Lard; Susan Lewis; Marc Lowenthal; Tom Parks; those among my architecture instructors who valued plain English; my students who have asked and answered so many of the questions that led to this book; and most of all my partner and agent, Sorche Fairbank.

101 Things I Learned in Architecture School

YES

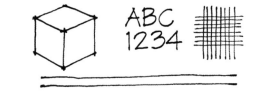

NO

How to draw a line

1 Architects use different lines for different purposes, but the line type most specific to architecture is drawn with an emphasis at the beginning and at the end. This practice anchors a line to the page and gives a drawing conviction and punch. If your lines trail off at the ends, your drawings will tend to look wimpy and vague. To train yourself to make strong lines, practice making a small blob or kickback at the beginning and end of every stroke.

2 Overlap lines slightly where they meet. This will keep corners from looking inappropriately rounded.

3 When sketching, don't "feather and fuzz" your way across the page—that is, don't make a vague-looking line out of many short, overlapping segments. Instead, move your pencil from start to end in a controlled, fluid motion. You might find it helpful to draw a light guide line before drawing your final line. Don't erase your guide lines when the drawing is complete—they will lend it character and life.

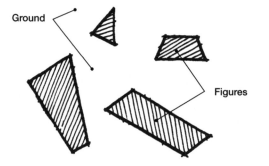

Ground

Figures

A *figure* is an element or shape placed on a page, canvas, or other background. *Ground* is the space of the page.

A figure is also called object, form, element, or positive shape. Ground is alternately called space, residual space, white space, or field.

4 figures arranged randomly with negative space resulting

The same 4 figures arranged to create positive space (a triangle)

The same 4 figures arranged to create positive space (the letter A)

Figure-ground theory states that the space that results from placing figures should be considered as carefully as the figures themselves.

Space is called *negative space* if it is unshaped after the placement of figures. It is *positive space* if it has a shape.

When elements or spaces are not explicit but are nonetheless apparent—we can see them even though we *can't* see them—they are said to be *implied*.

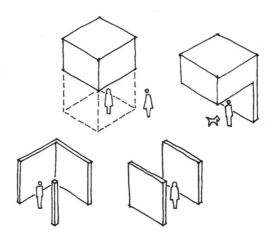

Solid-void theory is the three-dimensional counterpart to figure-ground theory. It holds that the volumetric spaces shaped or implied by the placement of solid objects are as important as, or more important than, the objects themselves.

A three-dimensional space is considered a positive space if it has a defined shape and a sense of boundary or threshold between in and out. Positive spaces can be defined in an infinite number of ways by points, lines, planes, solid volumes, trees, building edges, columns, walls, sloped earth, and innumerable other elements.

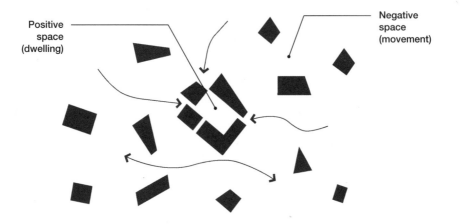

Positive space (dwelling)

Negative space (movement)

A college "quad" is usually the preferred space on a
campus for social interaction and hanging out.

We move through negative spaces and dwell in positive spaces.

The shapes and qualities of architectural spaces greatly influence human experience and behavior, for we inhabit the spaces of our built environment and not the solid walls, roofs, and columns that shape it. Positive spaces are almost always preferred by people for lingering and social interaction. Negative spaces tend to promote movement rather than dwelling in place.

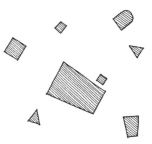

Medieval city
figure-ground plan

Contemporary suburb
figure-ground plan

Suburban buildings are freestanding objects *in* space. Urban buildings are often shapers *of* space.

When we create buildings today, we frequently focus our efforts on their shapes, with the shape of outdoor space a rather accidental leftover. These outdoor spaces, such as those typically found in suburbs, are negative spaces because the buildings aren't arranged to lend shape to the spaces in between.

Urban buildings, however, are often designed under the opposite assumptions: building shapes can be secondary to the shape of public space, to the extent that some urban buildings are almost literally "deformed" so that the plazas, courtyards, and squares that abut them may be given positive shape.

"Architecture is the thoughtful making of space."

—LOUIS KAHN

Vietnam Veterans War Memorial, Washington, D.C., 1982
Maya Lin, designer

Sense of place

Genius loci literally means genius of place. It is used to describe places that are deeply memorable for their architectural and experiential qualities.

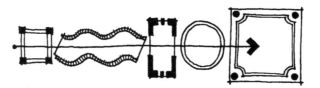

Our experience of an architectural space is strongly influenced by how we arrive in it.

A tall, bright space will feel taller and brighter if counterpointed by a low-ceilinged, softly lit space. A monumental or sacred space will feel more significant when placed at the end of a sequence of lesser spaces. A room with south-facing windows will be more strongly experienced after one passes through a series of north-facing spaces.

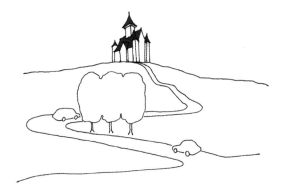

Use "denial and reward" to enrich passage through the built environment.

As we move through buildings, towns, and cities, we mentally connect visual cues from our surroundings to our needs and expectations. The satisfaction and richness of our experiences are largely the result of the ways in which these connections are made.

Denial and reward can encourage the formulation of a rich experience. In designing paths of travel, try presenting users a view of their target—a staircase, building entrance, monument, or other element—then momentarily screen it from view as they continue their approach. Reveal the target a second time from a different angle or with an interesting new detail. Divert users onto an unexpected path to create additional intrigue or even momentary lostness; then reward them with other interesting experiences or other views of their target. This additional "work" will make the journey more interesting, the arrival more rewarding.

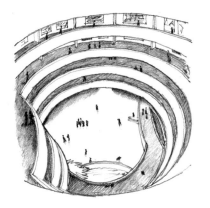

Guggenheim Museum, New York, 1959
Frank Lloyd Wright, architect

Design an architectural space to accommodate a *specific* program, experience, or intent.

Do not draw a rectangle—or any other arbitrary shape—on a floor plan, label it, and assume it will be suited to its intended use. Rather, investigate the program requirements in detail to determine the specifics of the activities that will take place there. Envision actual situations or experiences that will happen in those spaces, and design an architecture that accommodates and enhances them.

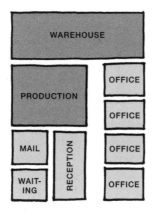

Space planning is the organizing or arranging of spaces to accommodate functional needs.

Space planning is a crucial skill for an architect, but arranging spaces to meet functional requirements explains only a little of what architects do. A space planner addresses the functional problem of fitting a building on its site; an architect is also concerned with the *meaning* of a site and its buildings. A space planner creates functional square footage for office workers; an architect considers the nature of the work performed in the office environment, its meaning to the workers, and its value to society. A space planner provides spaces for playing basketball, performing laboratory experiments, manufacturing widgets, or staging theatrical productions; an architect imbues the experience of these places with poignancy, richness, fun, beauty, and irony.

Architecture begins with an *idea*.

Good design solutions are not merely physically interesting but are driven by under-lying ideas. An idea is a specific mental structure by which we organize, understand, and give meaning to external experiences and information. Without underlying ideas informing their buildings, architects are merely *space planners*. Space planning with decoration applied to "dress it up" is not architecture; architecture resides in the DNA of a building, in an embedded sensibility that infuses its whole.

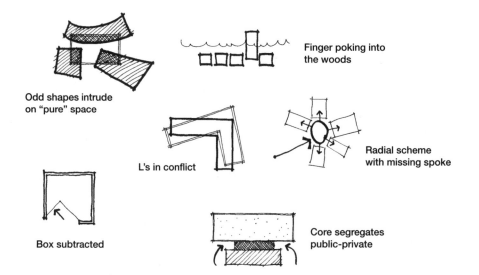

Odd shapes intrude
on "pure" space

Finger poking into
the woods

L's in conflict

Radial scheme
with missing spoke

Box subtracted

Core segregates
public-private

A *parti* is the central idea or concept of a building.

A *parti* [par-TEE] can be expressed several ways but is most often expressed by a diagram depicting the general floor plan organization of a building and, by implication, its experiential and aesthetic sensibility. A *parti* diagram can describe massing, entrance, spatial hierarchy, site relationship, core location, interior circulation, public/private zoning, solidity/transparency, and many other concerns. The proportion of attention given to each factor varies from project to project.

The *partis* shown here are from previously conceived projects; it is unlikely, if not impossible, to successfully carry a *parti* from an old project to a new project. The design process is the struggle to create a uniquely appropriate *parti* for a project.

Some will argue that an ideal *parti* is wholly inclusive—that it informs every aspect of a building from its overall configuration and structural system to the shape of the doorknobs. Others believe that a perfect *parti* is neither attainable nor desirable.

Parti derives from understandings that are nonarchitectural and must be cultivated before architectural form can be born.

At its most ambitious, *parti* derives from matters more transcendent than mere architecture. "L's in conflict," for example, might be a suitable *parti* for a new government building for two once-warring factions that have forged a new nation. "Finger poking into the woods" might derive from an ecological belief about the relationship between field and forest. "Missing spoke" might suggest a philosophy that loss invites opportunity.

The more specific a design idea is, the greater its appeal is likely to be.

Being nonspecific in an effort to appeal to everyone usually results in reaching no one. But drawing upon a specific observation, poignant statement, ironic point, witty reflection, intellectual connection, political argument, or idiosyncratic belief in a creative work can help you create environments others will identify with in their own way.

Design a flight of stairs for the day a nervous bride descends them. Shape a window to frame a view of a specific tree on a perfect day in autumn. Make a balcony for the worst dictator in the world to dress down his subjects. Create a seating area for a group of surly teenagers to complain about their parents and teachers.

Designing in idea-specific ways will not limit the ways in which people use and understand your buildings; it will give them license to bring their own interpretations and idiosyncrasies to them.

Any design decision should be justified in at least two ways.

A stair's primary purpose is to permit passage from floor to floor, but if well designed it can also serve as a congregation space, a sculptural element, and an orienting device in the building interior. A window can frame a view, bathe a wall with light, orient a building user to the exterior landscape, express the thickness of the wall, describe the structural system of the building, and acknowledge an axial relationship with another architectural element. A row of columns can provide structural support, define a circulation pathway, act as a "wayfinding" device, and serve as a rhythmic counterpoint to more irregularly placed architectural elements.

Opportunities for multiple design justifications can be found in almost every element of a building. The more justifications you can find or create for any element, the better.

19

Draw hierarchically.

When drawing in any medium, never work at a "100% level of detail" from one end of the sheet toward the other, blank end of the sheet. Instead, start with the most general elements of the composition and work gradually toward the more specific aspects of it. Begin by laying out the entire sheet. Use light guide lines, geometric alignments, visual gut-checks, and other methods to cross-check the proportions, relationships, and placement of the elements you are drawing. When you achieve some success at this schematic level, move to the next level of detail. If you find yourself focusing on details in a specific area of the drawing, indulge briefly, then move to other areas of the drawing. Evaluate your success continually, making local adjustments in the context of the entire sheet.

Engineers tend to be concerned with physical things in and of themselves. Architects are more directly concerned with the human interface with physical things.

An architect knows something about everything. An engineer knows everything about one thing.

An architect is a generalist, not a specialist—the conductor of a symphony, not a virtuoso who plays every instrument perfectly. As a practitioner, an architect coordinates a team of professionals that include structural and mechanical engineers, interior designers, building-code consultants, landscape architects, specifications writers, contractors, and specialists from other disciplines. Typically, the interests of some team members will compete with the interests of others. An architect must know enough about each discipline to negotiate and synthesize competing demands while honoring the needs of the client and the integrity of the entire project.

ABCDEFGHIJKLMNOPQR
STUVWXYZ 1234567890
abcdefghijklmnopqrstuvwxyz

Stylus

ABCDEFGHIJKLMNOPQRSTUVWXYZ
1234567890 abcdefghijklmnopqrstuvwxyz

City Blueprint

ABCDEFGHIJKLMNOPQRSTUVWXYZ
1234567890 abcdefghijklmnopqrstuvwxyz

Bernhard Fashion

ABCDEFGHIJKLMNOPQRSTUVWXYZ
1234567890 abcdefghijklmnopqrstuvwxyz

How to make architectural hand-lettering

Good architectural lettering adheres to several principles and techniques:

1 Honor legibility and consistency above all else.

2 Use guide lines (actual or imagined) to ensure uniformity.

3 Emphasize the beginning and end of all strokes, and overlap them slightly where they meet—just as in drawing lines.

4 Give your horizontal strokes a slight upward tilt. If they slope downward, your letters will look tired.

5 Give curved strokes a balloon-like fullness.

6 Give careful attention to the amount of white space between letters. An *E*, for example, will need more space when following an *I* than when coming after an *S* or *T*.

Several standard computer fonts are similar to architectural lettering and can serve as guides until you develop your manual lettering skills.

Objective engagement of reality
Detached observation

Subjective engagement of reality
Direct immersion

Reality may be engaged subjectively, by which one presumes a oneness with the objects of his concern, or objectively, by which a detachment is presumed.

Objectivity is the province of the scientist, technician, mechanic, logician, and mathematician. Subjectivity is the milieu of the artist, musician, mystic, and free spirit. Citizens of modern cultures are inclined to value the objective view—and hence it may tend to be your world view—but both modes of engagement are crucial to understanding and creating architecture.

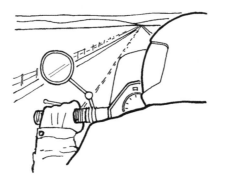

24

"Science works with chunks and bits and pieces of things with the continuity presumed, and [the artist] works only with the continuities of things with the chunks and bits and pieces presumed."

—ROBERT PIRSIG, *ZEN AND THE ART OF MOTORCYCLE MAINTENANCE*

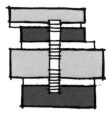

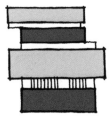

Stair across layers   Stair parallel to layers

Use your *parti* as a guidepost in designing the many aspects of a building.

25

When designing a stair, window, column, roof, lobby, elevator core, or any other aspect of a building, always consider how its design can express and reinforce the essential idea of the building.

Imagine, for example, a *parti* that is intended to express a layered organization, with each layer having unique architectural qualities. A central stair within this building could be:

1 oriented *across* the layers, so that one traverses the layers in traveling the stair;

2 parallel to the other layers, that is, a layer in and of itself;

3 left outside the layer system in order to preserve its purity;

4 anything else that helps say, "This building is about layers" (and nothing that says something contradictory).

Week 1   Week 2   Week 4

Week 7   Week 8   Week 10

Good designers are fast on their feet.

26

As the design process advances, complications inevitably arise—structural problems, fluctuating client requests, difficulties in resolving fire egress, pieces of the program forgotten and rediscovered, new understandings of old information, and much more. Your *parti*—once a wondrous prodigy—will suddenly face failure.

A poor designer will attempt to hold onto a failed *parti* and patch local fixes onto the problem areas, thus losing the integrity of the whole. Others may feel defeated and abandon the pursuit of an integrated whole. But a good designer understands the erosion of a *parti* as a helpful indication of where a project needs to go next.

When complications in the design process ruin your scheme, change—or if necessary, abandon—your *parti*. But don't abandon *having* a *parti,* and don't dig in tenaciously in defense of a scheme that no longer works. Create another *parti* that holistically incorporates all that you now know about the building.

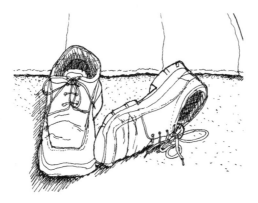

Soft ideas, soft lines; hard ideas, hard lines

27

Fat markers, charcoal, pastels, crayons, paint, soft pencils, and other loose or soft implements are valuable tools for exploring conceptual ideas early in the design process, as by their nature they tend to encourage broad thinking and deny fine-grained decisions. Fine-point markers and sharp pencils become more useful as the design process moves closer to a more highly resolved plan. Value drawings can help express nuances and subtleties.

Hard-line drawings—drawings drafted to scale with a straightedge or computer program—are best for conveying information that is decisive, specific, and quantitative, such as final floor plans or detailed wall sections. They can be occasionally useful in schematic design, such as when you need to test out the dimensional workability of a design concept. When overused as a design tool, however, computer drafting programs can encourage the endless generation of options rather than foster a deepening understanding of the design problem you wish to solve.

A good designer isn't afraid to throw away a good idea.

28

Just because an interesting idea occurs to you doesn't mean it belongs in the building you are designing. Subject every idea, brainstorm, random musing, and helpful suggestion to careful, critical consideration. Your goal as a designer should be to create an integrated whole, not to incorporate all the best features in your building whether or not they work together.

Think of a *parti* as an author employs a thesis, or as a composer employs a musical theme: not every idea a creator conjures up belongs in the work at hand! Save your good but ill-fitting ideas for another time and project—and with the knowledge that they might not work then, either.

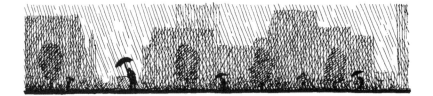

Being process-oriented, not product-driven, is the most important and difficult skill for a designer to develop.

Being process-oriented means:

1   seeking to understand a design problem before chasing after solutions;

2   not force-fitting solutions to old problems onto new problems;

3   removing yourself from prideful investment in your projects and being slow to fall in love with your ideas;

4   making design investigations and decisions holistically (that address several aspects of a design problem at once) rather than sequentially (that finalize one aspect of a solution before investigating the next);

5   making design decisions conditionally—that is, with the awareness that they may or may not work out as you continue toward a final solution;

6   knowing when to change and when to stick with previous decisions;

7   accepting as normal the anxiety that comes from not knowing what to do;

8   working fluidly between concept-scale and detail-scale to see how each informs the other;

9   always asking "What if . . . ?" regardless of how satisfied you are with your solution.

"A proper building grows naturally, logically, and poetically out of all its conditions."

—LOUIS SULLIVAN, *KINDERGARTEN CHATS* [PARAPHRASE]

Improved design process, not a perfectly realized building, is the most valuable thing you gain from one design studio and take with you to the next.

Design studio instructors, above all else, want their students to develop good process. If an instructor gives a good grade to what appears to you to be a poor project, it is probably because the student has demonstrated good process. Likewise, you may see an apparently good project receive a mediocre grade. Why? Because a project doesn't deserve a good grade if the process that led to it was sloppy, ill-structured, or the result of hit-and-miss good luck.

The most effective, most creative problem solvers engage in a process of meta-thinking, or "thinking about the thinking."

32

Meta-thinking means that you are aware of *how* you are thinking as you are *doing* the thinking. Meta-thinkers engage in continual internal dialogue of testing, stretching, criticizing, and redirecting their thought processes.

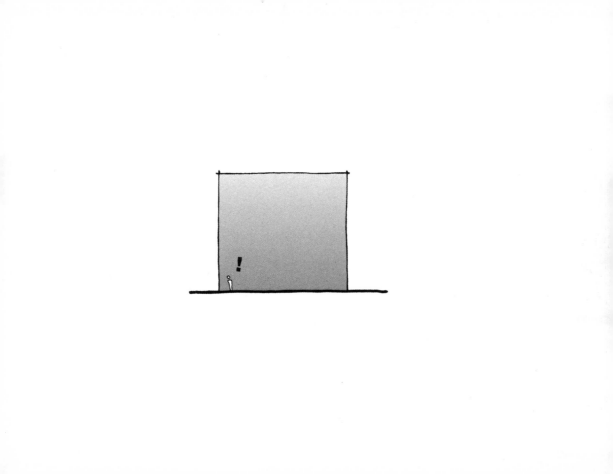

If you wish to imbue an architectural space or element with a particular quality, make sure that quality is really there.

If you want a wall to feel thick, make sure it is **THICK**.

If a space is to feel tall, make sure it really is TALL.

The clear demonstration of design intent is crucial for beginning designers. Experienced designers often know how to give great impact to subtle differentiations.

34

Frame a view, don't merely exhibit it.

Although a "wall of windows" might seem the best treatment for a dramatic view, richer experiences are often found in views that are discreetly selected, framed, screened, or even denied. As a designer, work to carefully shape, size, and place windows such that they are specific to the views and experiences they address.

35

"I like a view but I like to sit with my back turned to it."

—GERTRUDE STEIN, *THE AUTOBIOGRAPHY OF ALICE B. TOKLAS*

36

Value drawings (rendered in shade and
shadow) tend to convey emotions better
than line drawings.

Any aesthetic quality is usually enhanced by the presence of a counterpoint.

When seeking to bring a particular aesthetic quality (bright, dark, tall, smooth, straight, wiggly, proud, and the like) to a space, element, or building, try including an opposite or counterposing quality for maximum impact. If you want a room to feel tall and bright, try designing an approach through a low, dark space. If you want an atrium to feel like a geometrically pure, highly organized center of a building, surround it with spaces that are more organically or randomly organized. If you want to emphasize the richness of a material, counterpose it with a humble, less refined product. Every aspect of a building offers such opportunities: rough surfaces counterposed with smooth surfaces, horizontal masses with vertical masses, repetitive columns with continuous walls, linear arrangements with curves, large windows with small ones, top-lit spaces with side-lit spaces, flowing spaces with compartmentalized rooms, and so on.

37

The cardinal points of the compass offer associations of meaning that can enhance architectural experience.

EAST: youthfulness, innocence, freshness

SOUTH: activity, clarity, simplicity

WEST: aging, questioning, wisdom

NORTH: maturity, acceptance, death

Such associations, while not absolute, can help you decide where to locate various spaces and activities on a site or within a building: What might compass orientation suggest about the placement of a mortuary, a worship space, an adult education lecture hall, or an infant nursery?

A static composition appears to be at rest.

39

Static compositions are usually symmetrical. At their most successful, they suggest power, firmness, conviction, certainty, authority, and permanence. Less successful examples can be unengaging and boring.

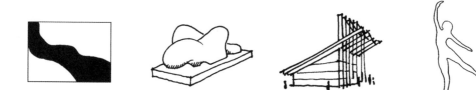

A dynamic composition encourages the eye to explore.

40

Dynamic compositions are almost always asymmetrical. They can suggest activity, excitement, fun, movement, flow, aggression, and conflict. Less successful examples can be jarring or disorienting.

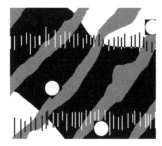

Moves and counterpoints

To create a dynamic, balanced composition in either 2D or 3D, make a strong initial design decision that is dynamic and unbalanced; then follow it with a secondary dynamic move that counterpoints the first move. Think of a counterpoint as a sort of aesthetic rebuttal: it is similar to but not quite the same as an opposite, as an infinite number of counterpoints can theoretically be made to a given move. A single, large swirl, for example, can be counterpointed by several small squares because "several" opposes "single" and "small" opposes "large." But that same swirl can also be counterpointed by choppy zigzag, by an emphatically regular grid, by a series of floating circles, and so on, because *each* countering move has qualities that are in some way opposite the qualities of the swirl.

In the composition at left, there are at least four different moves, each counterpointing all the other moves.

Those tedious first-year studio exercises in "spots and dots" and "lumps and bumps" really do have something to do with architecture.

Many beginning architecture students grow bored and impatient with the two- and three-dimensional design exercises commonly assigned in beginning design studios. And upper-level students, grateful to have survived beginning design, often fail to look back to their early design lessons to see how they can provide a foundation for solving complex architectural problems.

If your instructor isn't making clear the connection of 2D and 3D design to "real" architecture, ask for examples. Or ask an instructor in an upper level studio. A thorough grounding in the rudiments of 2D and 3D design will take you farthest in the long run through the complex field of architecture.

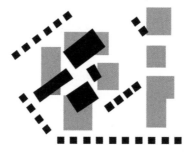

Site plan study for a college campus

When having difficulty resolving a floor plan, site plan, building elevation, section, or building shape, consider it as a 2D or 3D composition.

This will encourage you to give balanced attention to form and space, help you integrate disparate aspects of the scheme, and discourage you from focusing excessively on your pet features. Questions you can ask in 2D or 3D include:

- Does the composition have an overall balance?

- Is there a mixture of elements of different sizes and textures to attract the eye in different ways and from different distances?

- Is there a major "move" and one or more counterpoints?

- Do any areas of the composition appear to have been ignored?

43

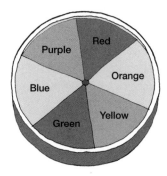

Color theory provides a framework for understanding the behavior and meaning of colors.

Colors may be associated with the seasons:

- **WINTER:** gray, white, ice blue, and similar colors

- **AUTUMN:** gold, russet, olive, brownish purple, muted or muddy tones

- **SUMMER:** primary or bright colors

- **SPRING:** pastel tones

44

Colors may be categorized as warm or cool. Cool colors tend to recede from the viewer—that is, they appear to be farther away, while warm colors advance.

- **WARM:** reds, browns, yellows, yellow- or olive-greens

- **COOL:** blues, grays, true- or blue-greens

A color wheel, on which colors located opposite are complementary, may be used to organize colors. Using complements together—for example, blue with orange—can help create a balanced color scheme.

Three levels of knowing

SIMPLICITY is the world view of the child or uninformed adult, fully engaged in his own experience and happily unaware of what lies beneath the surface of immediate reality.

COMPLEXITY characterizes the ordinary adult world view. It is characterized by an awareness of complex systems in nature and society but an inability to discern clarifying patterns and connections.

INFORMED SIMPLICITY is an enlightened view of reality. It is founded upon an ability to discern or create clarifying patterns within complex mixtures. *Pattern recognition* is a crucial skill for an architect, who must create a highly ordered building amid many competing and frequently nebulous design considerations.

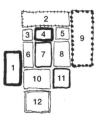

Simplicity

3 elements used to
create 3 spaces

Complexity created through
excessive agglomeration

12 elements required to
create 12 spaces

Complexity created through
informed simplicity

3 elements combined to
create 12 spaces

Create architectural richness through *informed simplicity* or an *interaction of simples* rather than through unnecessarily busy agglomerations.

Whether an architectural aesthetic is intended to be minimalist or complex, its experience mysterious or clear, its spaces Spartan or richly layered, a building must be a highly ordered thing. Creating simplifying patterns in a building plan is a way of lending order while allowing multiple readings and experiences.

Some examples of unnecessary complexity:

- making a dozen separate design moves when three well-informed moves can accomplish as much;

- busying up a project with doodads because it is boring without them;

- agglomerating many unrelated elements without concern for their unity because they are interesting in themselves.

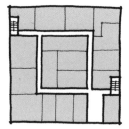

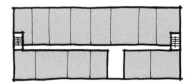

Square buildings, building wings, and rooms can be difficult to organize.

Because a square is inherently nondynamic, it doesn't naturally suggest movement. This can make it difficult to establish appropriate circulation pathways in a square floor plan. Further, interior rooms in square buildings can be far removed from natural light and air. Nonsquare shapes—rectangles, crescents, wedges, ells, and so on— more naturally accommodate patterns of movement, congregation, and habitation.

This project
wants to be
about a
complexity of
multiplicities

But certainly
a multiplicity of
similars would
better reflect the
perturbance of
the modularity,
given the
particularity
of the language
established
by the axial
relationships

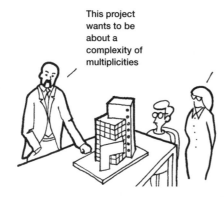

If you can't explain your ideas to your grandmother in terms that she understands, you don't know your subject well enough.

48

Some architects, instructors, and students use overly complex (and often meaningless!) language in an attempt to gain recognition and respect. You might have to let some of them get away with it, but don't imitate them. Professionals who know their subject area well know how to communicate their knowledge to others in everyday language.

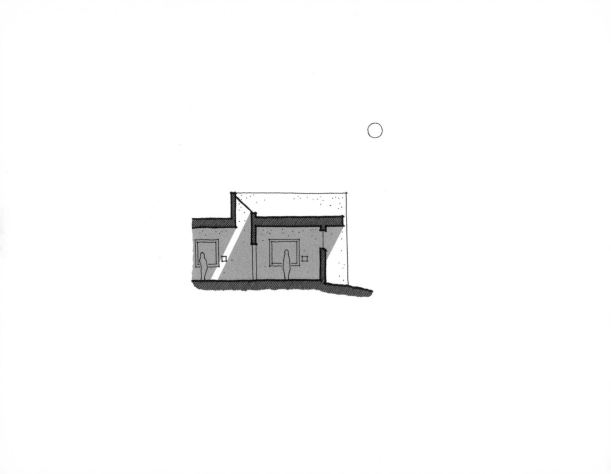

The altitude, angle, and color of daylighting varies with compass orientation and time of day. In the northern hemisphere:

Daylight from **NORTH**-facing windows tends to be shadowless, diffuse, and neutral or slightly grayish most of the day and year.

Daylight from the **EAST** is strongest in the morning. It tends to be of low altitude, with soft, long shadows, and gray-yellow in color.

Daylight from the **SOUTH** is dominant from late morning to mid-afternoon. It tends to render colors accurately and cast strong, crisp shadows.

Daylight from the **WEST** is strongest in the late afternoon and early evening and has a rich gold-orange cast. It can penetrate deeply into buildings and occasionally be overbearing.

49

Windows look dark in the daytime.

When rendering an exterior building view, making the windows dark (except when the glass is reflective or a light-colored blind or curtain is behind the glass) will add depth and realism.

50

Jaguar E-type

Beauty is due more to harmonious relationships among the elements of a composition than to the elements themselves.

Put on your favorite pants, sharpest shirt, and coolest jacket without regard for their coordination. Then walk down the street and try not to get laughed at.

Build a car out of the most beautiful features of the most stunning cars ever made. See if your friends will be seen in it with you.

Create a dream lover out of body parts from your favorite Hollywood hotties. See if you're as turned on by the sum of the parts as you were by the previous wholes.

It's the *dialogue* of the pieces, not the pieces themselves, that creates aesthetic success.

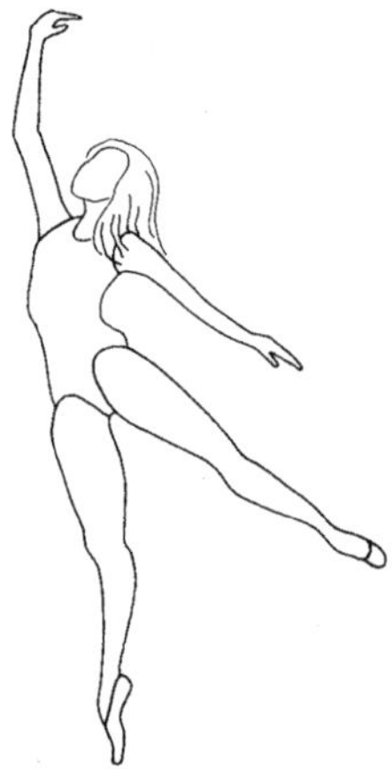

An appreciation for asymmetrical balance is considered by many to demonstrate a capacity for higher-order thinking.

Whether creating a static or dynamic composition, an artist usually seeks to achieve balance. Balance is inherent in a symmetrical composition, but asymmetrical compositions can be either balanced or unbalanced. Consequently, asymmetry tends to require a more complex and sophisticated understanding of wholeness.

A good building reveals different things about itself when viewed from different distances.

53

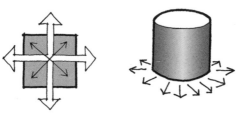

Geometric shapes have inherent dynamic qualities that influence our perception and experience of the built environment.

A square, for example, is inherently static and nondirectional. Consequently, a room of square or cubic proportions may feel restful, although if not carefully designed it can feel dull or vacuous. A rectangle, because it has two long sides and two shorter sides, is inherently directional. The longer a rectangular room is, the more it will encourage visual and physical movement parallel to its long axis.

A circle has an infinite number of radii and is therefore both omnidirectional and nondirectional: a round or cylindrical building addresses every surrounding point equally and therefore can be an effective focal point on the landscape. At the same time, no aspect of a circular building is inherently the front, side, or rear.

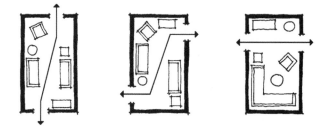

54

Undesirable circulation
Through-traffic bisects
seating area

Good circulation
Primary seating area is
protected from traffic

The best placement of a circulation path through a small room is usually straight through, a few feet from one wall.

This allows the primary users of the room to be uninterrupted by through-traffic. The worst circulation through a small room is usually a path running diagonally through it or parallel to its long axis. Comfortable furniture arrangements are difficult to achieve under such circumstances, as persons dwelling in the space will tend to feel—if not in fact be—in the way of those passing through.

55

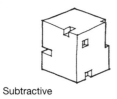

Subtractive

Abstract/mixed

Thorncrown Chapel
Additive, symmetrical

Fallingwater
Additive, asymmetrical

Notre Dame du Haut
Addition of shaped/molded forms;
windows subtracted or "punched"

Guggenheim Bilbao
Addition of shaped/molded forms

Most architectural forms can be classified as additive, subtractive, shaped, or abstract.

ADDITIVE FORMS appear to have been assembled from individual pieces.

SUBTRACTIVE FORMS appear to have been carved or cut from a previously "whole" form.

SHAPED OR MOLDED FORMS appear to have been formed from a plastic material through directly applied force.

ABSTRACT FORMS are of uncertain origin.

An effective oral presentation of a studio project begins with the general and proceeds toward the specific.

1 State the design problem assigned.

2 Discuss the values, attitude, and approach you brought to the design problem.

3 Describe your design process and the major discoveries and ideas you encountered along the way.

4 State the *parti,* or unifying concept, that emerged from your process. Illustrate this with a simple diagram.

5 Present your drawings (plans, sections, elevations, and vignettes) and models, always describing them in relationship to the *parti*.

6 Perform a modest and confident self-critique.

Never begin a presentation by saying, "Well, you go in the front door here" unless your goal is to put your audience to sleep.

The proportions of a building are an aesthetic statement of how it was built.

Traditional architecture (built prior to the advent of modern construction methods in the late 1800s) tends to have short structural spans and vertical window proportions. Modern buildings more often have long spans and horizontal window proportions.

The vertical proportions of traditional buildings were due to the length of a stone or wood lintel (the supporting beam over an opening) being limited to what could be found, fabricated, and lifted into place by hand. The only way to make a large window when its width is limited is to make it tall.

Contemporary steel and concrete construction methods allow long structural spans, so windows in contemporary buildings can have any proportion. Often they are given horizontal proportions, however, at least in part because this distinguishes them aesthetically from traditional windows.

Monadnock Building, Chicago, 1891
Burnham and Root, architects

Traditional buildings have thick exterior walls. Modern buildings have thin walls.

Traditional architecture uses the exterior walls to support the weight of the building. The walls must be thick because they receive heavy loads from the floors, roof, and walls above them, which they then transfer to the earth. The exterior walls of the twelve-story Monadnock Building, for example, are six feet thick at the base.

Most modern buildings employ a frame of steel or concrete columns and beams to support structural loads and transfer the building's weight to the earth. The exterior walls are attached to and supported by this frame, and therefore serve as a barrier against the weather only. Thus, the walls can be much thinner than those of traditional buildings, and—despite appearances—they usually do not rest on the ground. When brick or stone is used to clad a skyscraper, for example, the masonry walls are not piled up on the ground for forty stories, but are supported by the super-structure every story or two.

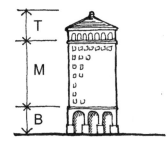
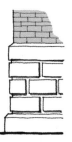

Traditional architecture employs a tripartite, or base-middle-top, format.

The base of a traditional building is usually designed to express its structural support of the upper stories and the transfer of those loads to the ground. A masonry base is typically *rusticated*—the stones and mortar joints are shaped in a way that suggests the base is quite heavy and thick. The top of a traditional building is symbolically a crown or hat that announces on the skyline the building's purpose or spirit.

60

Farnsworth House, Plano, Illinois, 1951
Mies van der Rohe, architect

"Less is more."

—LUDWIG MIES VAN DER ROHE

61

Vanna Venturi House, Philadelphia, Pennsylvania, 1962
Robert Venturi, architect

"Less is a bore."

—ROBERT VENTURI,
LEARNING FROM LAS VEGAS

62

When introducing floor level changes, avoid the "Dick Van Dyke step."

One step between floor levels is rarely sufficient to create a meaningful differentiation of space. Often, it is an inconvenient people-tripper that can result in lawsuits. A three-step differentiation is usually the minimum that feels right.

63

NOTE: Dick Van Dyke is a comedic television actor known for awkward pratfalls.

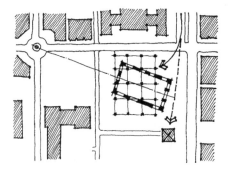

If you rotate or skew a floor plan, column grid, or other aspect of a building, make it mean something.

Placing columns, spaces, walls, or other architectural elements off-geometry because you have seen it done in fashionable architecture magazines is a poor design justification. Doing so to create a gathering place, direct a circulation path, focus an entry, open a vista, acknowledge a monument, accommodate a street geometry, address the sun, or point the way to Mecca are better reasons.

64

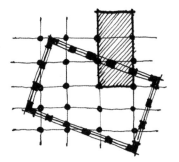

Always show structural columns on your floor plans—even very early in the design process.

Showing a structural system on your floor plans throughout the design process—even if nothing more than a few dots or blobs—will help you organize the program, encourage you to think of your creation as a real building, and help you control the eventual structural resolution. Indeed, an architect who doesn't adequately consider structure may have an undesirable structural system imposed on the building by a structural engineer.

The placement and spacing of columns are usually regularized for visual unity and construction efficiency. Ordinary wood frame buildings typically have a column line or bearing wall every 10 to 18 feet; commercial-scale buildings of steel or concrete, every 25 to 50 feet. Structural systems for exhibit halls, arenas, and other such spaces can have spans of 90 feet or more.

65

Saint Peter's Basilica, Rome, built 1506–1615
Donato Bramante, architect

Columns are not merely structural elements; they are tools for organizing and shaping space.

Although their primary purpose is of course structural, columns are invaluable in other ways: a row of columns can define the spaces on one side as different from those on the other side; distinguish circulation pathways from gathering spaces; act as a "wayfinding" element in a building interior; or serve as a rhythmic element on a building exterior.

Different column shapes have different spatial effects: square columns are directionally neutral; rectangular columns establish "grain" or directionality; and round columns contribute to a flowing sense of space. Complex column shapes were often employed in traditional masonry architecture to create richly interwoven spaces.

A good graphic presentation meets the Ten-Foot Test.

The essential elements of the drawings you pin up for a design studio presentation—in particular, labels and titles—should be legible from 10 feet away.

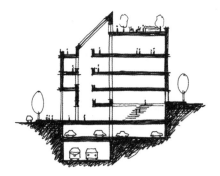

Design in section!

Good designers work back and forth between plans and sections, allowing each to inform the other. Poor designers fixate on floor plans and draw building sections afterward as a record of decisions already made in plan. But sections, it could be said, represent 50 percent of the experience of a building. In fact, some sites (such as those with steep slopes) and building types (those requiring tall interior spaces, careful management of connections between floors, or unusual attention to daylighting) require that you design in section *before* you think about floor plans.

68

Random Unsubstantiated Hypothesis

A floor plan demonstrates the organizational logic of a building; a section embodies its emotional experience.

69

Design in perspective!

Architects are expert at reading and interpreting orthographic (plan, section, and elevation) drawings, but even the best cannot understand everything about a building this way. Sketching accurate one- and two-point perspectives of your buildings and building interiors throughout the design process will allow you to test your expectations of how your building will look, work, and feel in actual experience and to visualize design opportunities not evident in two-dimensional drawings.

70

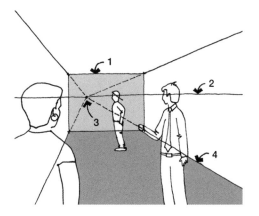

How to sketch a one-point perspective of a rectangular interior space:

1 Draw the end wall of the room in correct proportion. In the example, the end wall is 8 feet high by 12 feet wide, so its width is one and a half times its height.

2 Lightly draw a horizon line (HL) across the page. The HL is the height of your eye above the floor. If you are 5 feet 6 inches tall, the HL will be about 5 feet (five-eighths of the way) up the wall.

3 Mark a vanishing point (VP) on the horizon line. The VP represents your location, as the viewer of the scene, relative to the side walls. Here, the viewer/VP has been established 3 feet from the left-hand wall.

4 Lightly draw lines from the VP through the four corners of the end wall, then extend them more heavily toward the edges of the paper. The heavier portions of these lines depict the outer limits of the space.

5 To include a person of similar height to the viewer, place the center of his or her head on the horizon line, then increase or decrease the size of the person for foreground or background placement.

Design with models!

Three-dimensional models—both material and electronic—can help you understand your project in new ways. The most useful model for designing is the building massing model—a quick material (clay, cardboard, foam, plastic, sheet metal, found objects, and so on) study by which you can easily compare and test design options under consideration.

Carefully crafted, highly detailed finish models are not useful as design tools, as their purpose is to document design decisions already made rather than help evaluate ideas under consideration.

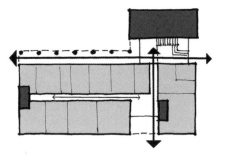

The two most important keys to effectively organizing a floor plan are managing solid-void relationships and resolving circulation.

For conceptual design purposes, consider the core functions of a building—its toilet rooms, storage rooms, mechanical spaces, elevator shafts, fire stairs, and the like—to be solids. Core spaces are usually grouped together or located near each other. Voids are the larger, primary program spaces of a building—its lobbies, laboratories, worship spaces, exhibit galleries, library reading rooms, assembly halls, gymnasiums, living rooms, offices, manufacturing spaces, and so on. Solving a floor plan means creating practical and pleasing relationships between core spaces and primary program spaces.

A building's circulation—where people walk—should interconnect the program spaces with the stairs and elevator lobbies in a way that is both logical and interesting: the circulation system has to work both efficiently (particularly in event of fire) and aesthetically, offering pleasant surprises, unexpected vistas, intriguing nooks, agreeable lighting variations, and other interesting experiences along the way.

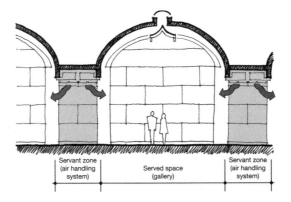

Kimbell Art Museum, Fort Worth, Texas, 1972
Louis Kahn, architect

Many of the building types assigned in architectural design studios, such as museums, libraries, and assembly buildings, can be effectively organized by Louis Kahn's notion of "served" and "servant" spaces.

Served/servant spaces are analogous to program/core spaces. Kahn expertly grouped servant spaces in a way that met the functional needs of the building while lending quietly poetic rhythms to the whole.

74

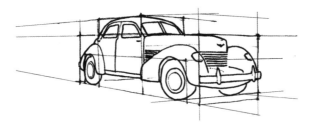

Draw the box it came in.

Buildings, because they have hard edges and are frequently rectilinear, lend themselves to simple line drawings. However, many of the things that architects draw—cars, furniture, trees, people—are nonrectilinear. When an object seems too complex to draw, first draw the box you imagine it came in. Then draw the object within that simplified container.

Overdesign.

At the outset of the design process, make your spaces about 10 percent larger than they need to be to meet the assigned program. During the design process, additional spatial requirements will arise—for mechanical rooms, structural columns, storage, circulation space, wall thicknesses, and a hundred other things not anticipated when the building program was created.

The point of overdesigning is not to design a larger building than is necessary but to design one that is ultimately the right size. In the unlikely event the extra space turns out to be unnecessary, you will find it easier to shrink an overlarge building than to create more space where it doesn't already exist.

Façade detail, Simmons Hall, Massachusetts Institute of Technology, 2002
Steven Holl, architect

No design system is or should be perfect.

Designers are often hampered by a well-intentioned but erroneous belief that a good design solution is perfectly systematic and encompasses all aspects of a design problem without exception. But nonconforming oddities can be enriching, humanizing aspects of your project. Indeed, exceptions to the rule are often more interesting than the rules themselves.

77

"The success of the masterpieces seems to lie not so much in their freedom from faults—indeed we tolerate the grossest errors in them all—but in the immense persuasiveness of a mind which has completely mastered its perspective."

—VIRGINIA WOOLF,
"THE DEATH OF THE MOTH"

78

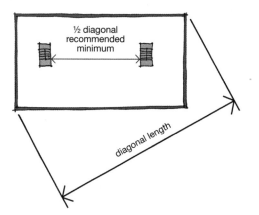

Always place fire stairs at opposite ends of the buildings you design, even in the earliest stages of the design process.

It is easy to think that a designer has more glamorous concerns than fire stairs, but emergency egress has everything to do with the more general workings of a building. If you don't ingrain such safety considerations into your design process, you can expect to defend your disinterest before a judge and jury one day.

79

Cool drawing titles for schematic design

Use a light-colored marker with a big chisel point to form lowercase architectural letters; then trace around the resulting shapes with a thin black pen.

80

Properly gaining control of the design process tends to feel like one is *losing* control of the design process.

The design process is often structured and methodical, but it is not a mechanical process. Mechanical processes have predetermined outcomes, but the creative process strives to produce something that has not existed before. Being genuinely creative means that you don't know where you are going, even though you are responsible for shepherding the process. This requires something different from conventional, authoritarian control; a loose velvet tether is more likely to help.

Engage the design process with patience. Don't imitate popular portrayals of the creative process as depending on a singular, pell-mell rush of inspiration. Don't try to solve a complex building in one sitting or one week. Accept uncertainty. Recognize as normal the feeling of lostness that attends to much of the process. Don't seek to relieve your anxiety by marrying yourself prematurely to a design solution; design divorces are never pretty.

True architectural style does not come from a conscious effort to create a particular look. It results obliquely—even accidentally—out of a holistic process.

The builder of an American colonial house in 1740 did not think, as we often do today, "I really like colonials, I think I'll build one." Rather, houses were built sensibly with the materials and technology available, and with an eye sensitively attuned to proportion, scale, and harmony. Colonial windows had small, multiple panes of glass not because of a desire to make a colonial-looking window, but because the technology of the day could produce and transport only small sheets of glass with consistency. Shutters were functional, not decorative; they were closed over windows when needed to provide shade from the sun. The colonial architecture that resulted from these considerations was uncalculated: Early American houses were colonial because the *colonists* were colonial.

All design endeavors express the zeitgeist.

Zeitgeist is a German word meaning, roughly, the spirit of an age. The zeitgeist is the prevailing ethos or sensibility of an era, the general mood of its people, the tenor of public discourse, the flavor of daily life, the intellectual inclinations and biases that underlie human endeavor. Because of the zeitgeist, parallel (although not identical) trends tend to occur in literature, religion, science, architecture, art, and other creative enterprises.

It is impossible to rigidly define the eras of human history; however, we can summarize the primary intellectual trends in the West as follows:

- **ANCIENT ERA:** a tendency to accept myth-based truths;

- **CLASSICAL (GREEK) ERA:** a valuing of order, rationality, and democracy;

- **MEDIEVAL ERA:** a dominance of the truths of organized religion;

- **RENAISSANCE:** holistic embracings of science and art;

- **MODERN ERA:** a favoring of truths revealed by the scientific method;

83

- **POSTMODERN (CURRENT) ERA:** an inclination to hold that truth is relative or impossible to know.

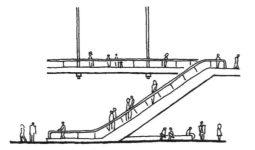

Two points of view on architecture

ARCHITECTURE IS AN EXERCISE IN *TRUTH*. A proper building is responsible to universal knowledge and is wholly honest in the expression of its functions and materials.

ARCHITECTURE IS AN EXERCISE IN *NARRATIVE*. Architecture is a vehicle for the telling of stories, a canvas for relaying societal myths, a stage for the theater of everyday life.

84

Balcony
Antibes, France

Gently suggest material qualities rather than draw them in a literal manner.

Architectural drawings, whether hand- or computer-generated, will look cartoonish if you make bricks "Brick Red" and roofs "Asphalt Black." Try using washed out or dulled-down colors that are more suggestive than literal. Likewise, don't draw every brick in a brick wall, every shingle on a shingled roof, or every tile in a tile floor. Selectively hint at material qualities.

85

Manage your ego.

If you want to be recognized for designing a good or even great building, forget about what *you* want the building to be; instead ask, "What does the *building* want to be?" A design problem has to be addressed on its own terms: the needs of the client, the nature of the site, the realities of the building program, and many others. These factors point toward an inherent order that must be acknowledged before self-expression can enter the design process.

Strive to accommodate and express universal concerns in your work—the human quest for meaning and purpose, the variegated play of light and shadow on a textured wall, the interweaving of public and private relationships, the structural and aesthetic opportunities inherent in building materials—and you will find an interested audience.

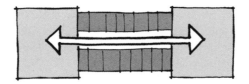

Careful anchor placement can generate an active building interior.

Anchors are program elements that inherently draw people to them. Department stores, for example, are located at opposite ends of a shopping mall because they draw many visitors. People walking between these large stores become window shoppers of the smaller stores in between. In this way, a seemingly inefficient relationship between the anchor stores fosters economic activity and interior street life.

Are there any anchor opportunities in your project? Try locating the entrance and locker rooms of a gymnasium at opposite ends of a recreation center. Place the registration desk and elevators in a hotel a little farther apart than is most efficient. Locate the access points for a parking garage and office lobby at a greater distance than might otherwise be considered ideal. In the spaces between, create interesting architectural experiences for your captive audience!

87

An object, surface, or space usually will feel more balanced or whole when its secondary articulation runs counter to its primary geometry.

Try striating a rectangular surface across its short dimension rather than parallel to its primary axis. Break down a long hallway with crossing elements. Try articulating a curved space radially rather than concentrically. When laying out floor tiles, see if orienting their long axis to the short axis of the room feels best.

88

Fabric buildings, or background buildings, are the more numerous buildings of a city. Object or foreground buildings are buildings of unusual importance.

Fabric buildings are buildings used for ordinary residences and commerce. In successful cities, fabric buildings form a physically cohesive texture that is indicative of an underlying social fabric. Object buildings are churches, mosques, government buildings, prominent residences, civic monuments, and similar structures. They tend to stand slightly or even dramatically apart from their context.

Roll your drawings for transport or storage with the image side facing *out*.

This will help them stay flat when you lay them on a table or pin them to a wall for display.

Build to the street wall.

When designing an urban infill building, place the front of it at the prevailing building line of the street unless there is a compelling reason to do otherwise. Indeed, it can be tempting, as it was for many modernist architects, to distinguish an urban building by pulling it back from the street, but urban life is predicated on proximity, walkability, and immediacy. Setting buildings back from the sidewalk makes them less accessible to passersby, reduces the economic viability of first floor businesses, and weakens the spatial definition of the street.

91

"Always design a thing by considering it in its next larger context—a chair in a room, a room in a house, a house in an environment, an environment in a city plan."

—ELIEL SAARINEN

92

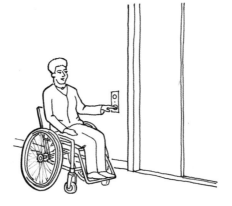

The primary mechanisms by which the government regulates the design of buildings are zoning laws, building codes, and accessibility codes.

ZONING CODES are generally concerned with how a building relates to its surroundings. They typically regulate use (residential, commercial, industrial, and so on), height, density, lot size, setbacks from property lines, and parking.

BUILDING CODES are primarily concerned with how a building works in and of itself. They regulate such features as building materials, floor area (larger for less flammable building materials), height (taller for less flammable materials), energy usage, fire protection systems, natural lighting, ventilation, and other such concerns.

ACCESSIBILITY CODES provide for the use of buildings by persons with physical challenges. They regulate ramps, stairs, handrails, toilet facilities, signage, heights of countertops and switches, and other such features. The national accessibility code is the ADA (Americans with Disabilities Act) Code. Most of the individual fifty states also have their own accessibility codes.

Longaberger Basket Building, Newark, Ohio, 1997
NBBJ Architects

A *duck* is a building that projects its meaning in a literal way.

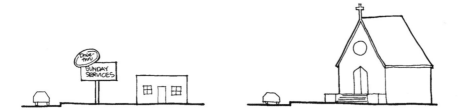

Meaning conveyed by signage   Meaning conveyed by
                                                architectural symbol

With regards to Robert Venturi

A *decorated shed* is a conventional building form that conveys meaning through signage or architectural ornament.

Summer people are 22 inches wide.
Winter people are 24 inches wide.

Limitations encourage creativity.

Never rue the limitations of a design problem—a too-small site, an inconvenient topography, an overlong space, an unfamiliar palate of materials, contradictory requests from the client ... Within those limitations lies the solution to the problem!

Does a steeply sloping site make it difficult to create a conventional building? Then celebrate the vertical relationships of spaces with a fascinating stair, ramp, or atrium. Does an ugly old wall face your building? Find ways to frame views of it so it becomes interesting and memorable. Have you been asked to design within a site, building, or room that is narrow and overlong? Turn those proportions into an interesting journey with a great payoff at the end.

97

The Chinese symbol for crisis is comprised of two characters: one indicating "danger," the other, "opportunity."

A design problem is not something to be overcome, but an opportunity to be embraced. The best design solutions do not make a problem go away, but accept the problem as a necessary state of the world. Frequently they are little more than an eloquent restatement of the problem.

Just do *something*.

When a design problem is so overwhelming as to be nearly paralyzing, don't wait for clarity to arrive before beginning to draw. Drawing is not simply a way of depicting a design solution; it is itself a way of learning about the problem you are trying to solve.

Give it a name.

When you come up with a concept, *parti,* or stray idea, give it a name. "Half-eaten donut," "eroded cube," "cleaved mass," "meeting of strangers," and other such monikers will help you explain to yourself what you have created. As the design process evolves and stronger concepts surface, allow new pet names to emerge and your old pet names to grow obsolete.

100

Zaha Hadid
b. 1950

Architects are late bloomers.

Most architects do not hit their professional stride until around age 50!

There is perhaps no other profession that requires one to integrate such a broad range of knowledge into something so specific and concrete. An architect must be knowledgeable in history, art, sociology, physics, psychology, materiality, symbology, political process, and innumerable other fields, and must create a building that meets regulatory codes, keeps out the weather, withstands earthquakes, has functioning elevators and mechanical systems, and meets the complex functional and emotional needs of its users. Learning to integrate so many concerns into a cohesive product takes a long time, with lots of trial and error along the way.

If you're going to be in the field of architecture, be in it for the long haul. It's worth it.

Matthew Frederick is an architect and urban designer who lives in Cambridge, Massachusetts. He has taught at a number of colleges and universities, including Boston Architectural College and Wentworth Institute of Technology.